HEAVENLY ANGEL

LAY LAY

EXPLAINS

WHICH BIBLE TO READ, WHICH BIBLE NOT TO READ, AND WHY

PUBLISHING COMPANY

ISBN: 978-0-6151-7484-6

www.crossover-ministries-publishing.com

TABLE OF CONTENTS

WHICH BIBLE TO READ, WHICH BIBLE NOT TO READ, AND WHY

JACOB AND JOSEPH

BIBLIOGRAPHY

ABOUT THE AUTHOR

I was dedicated to Jesus Christ of Nazareth as an infant and accepted Him as my Lord and Savior around seven years old when a visiting youth group led me in prayer at the alter. During my Salvation Prayer I asked Jesus to use me in a special ministry. Something that very few other Christians would want to do. I saw all the people just sitting in the pews, the ushers, and the Sunday School teachers and realized any Christian could do that. I wanted something different. One day in church service there was a visiting minister at a church I was visiting as well. The Minister said, "Jesus is going to make you a 'Healer of a Heart'". Then he asked me if I knew what that meant. I said, "No." the minister said, "I don't either, but whatever it is, Jesus is going to use you in a powerful way.

Helping Rachael, Jesus showed me what a 'Healer of the Heart' is. During the course of me helping Rachael to the 'Promised Land', a real Heavenly Angel named Lay Lay and I were allowed one hour one day to talk about Spiritual and Family situations from the King James Version of the Word of God. These books are designed to answer a lot of Spiritual Questions not even your minister can answer or your Church Denomination. I know theology Doctors who can't tell you how people other than Noah and his family made it past the 'Great Flood', yet their names are listed in the King James Version of the Word of God right after the 'World Wide Flood'. These books explain that and much more. I have written these books to tell the whole truth about the Word of God no matter how difficult it may be for me or others. Yes, there are things I write in these books that I don't even like, but in all fairness and total honestly, I must say the WHOLE TRUTH. The title of this book is 100% real. HEAVENLY ANGEL LAY LAY explained to me the differences of the bibles on the market today and which ones comes from Jesus Christ of Nazareth, which ones come from Religious Unclean Spirits and why.

INTRODUCTION

The first section of this book contains two excerpts from my book MATTHEW'S WORD 'TWO':REAL WORD OF GOD BIBLE when I was talking to Heavenly Angel Lay Lay and what Lay Lay told me about which bibles are Real Word of God Bibles on the market today. The second section of this book contains the rest of the life of Jacob (Also Known As Israel) and Joseph. All scriptures are take from the King James Version of the Word of God.

BOOKS WRITTEN BY WALTER BURCHETT, BA:

MATTHEW'S WORD 'TWO':REAL WORD OF GOD BIBLE   ISBN: 1-4116-6995-9

HEAVENLY ANGEL LAY LAY EXPLAINS WHY ADAM WAS NEVER CURSED
                                                                                                  ISBN: 978-1-84728-176-0

HEAVENLY ANGEL LAY LAY EXPLAINS WHY ABORTED BABIES DO NOT GO TO HEAVEN
                                                                                                  ISBN: 978-0-6151-7470-9

HEAVENLY ANGEL LAY LAY EXPLAINS THE BIBLICAL GROUNDS FOR MARRIAGE,
          SEPARATION, AND DIVORCE   ISBN: 978-0-6151-7481-5

HEAVENLY ANGEL LAY LAY EXPLAINS WHY PROFESSIONAL COUNSELORS HAVE 'HARDENED
          HEARTS'   ISBN: 978-0-6151-7482-2

HEAVENLY ANGEL LAY LAY EXPLAINS THE DIFFERENCE BETWEEN A 'COLD CHRISTIAN' AND
          A 'BACKSLIDER'   ISBN: 978-0-6151-7483-9

HEAVENLY ANGEL LAY LAY EXPLAINS WHICH BIBLE TO READ, WHICH BIBLE NOT TO READ,
          AND WHY   ISBN: 978-0-6151-7484-6

HEAVENLY ANGEL LAY LAY EXPLAINS WHY GAYS, LESBIANS, BI-SEXUALS, AND
          TRANSSEXUALS DO NOT GO TO HEAVEN   ISBN: 978-0-6151-7485-3

HEAVENLY ANGEL LAY LAY EXPLAINS WHY CHILDREN AND SPORTS ARE DEFINITELY A
          RELIGION IN TODAY'S SOCIETY   ISBN: 978-0-6151-7486-0

HEAVENLY ANGEL LAY LAY EXPLAINS WHAT 'MANY ARE CALLED, BUT FEW ARE CHOSEN
          REALLY MEANS   ISBN: 978-0-6151-7487-7

HEAVENLY ANGEL LAY LAY AND GUARDIAN ANGEL SHADOW GUESS THE REAL AGE OF THE
          EARTH   ISBN: 978-0-6151-7488-4

AN ABUSED MAN'S BATTLES, TRYING TO PROTECT HIS BOYS   ISBN: 978-0-6151-5191-5

HEAVENLY ANGEL LAY LAY

EXPLAINS

WHICH BIBLE TO READ, WHICH BIBLE NOT TO READ, AND WHY

WHICH BIBLE TO READ,
WHICH BIBLE NOT TO READ,
AND WHY

The following is an excerpt from my book called, **MATTHEW'S WORD 'TWO':REAL WORD OF GOD BIBLE**. This is one of the Bible Mysteries Heavenly Angel Lay Lay shared with me on our way, taking Rachael to the Promised Land. Since a Heavenly Angel told me this, how can I change anything that any Heavenly Angel said and make it better? If you don't know who Heavenly Angel Lay Lay is or how I was allowed to work with three different Heavenly Angels, then you will need to purchase **MATTHEW'S WORD 'TWO':REAL WORD OF GOD BIBLE** and read it (ISBN: 1-4116-6995-9). The first half of **MATTHEW'S WORD 'TWO':REAL WORD OF GOD BIBLE** is about how I was allowed to work with three different Heavenly Angels to begin with. The second half of **MATTHEW'S WORD 'TWO':REAL WORD OF GOD BIBLE** contains about 100 pages of Biblical facts Heavenly Angel Lay Lay was allowed to share with me. You will need to read the whole book in order to understand how I was allowed to work with three different Heavenly Angels for a little over a year of my life. Lay Lay explained to me why Adam didn't stop Eve from eating the 'forbidden fruit', what caused Cain to get so angry he killed Abel, what happened to the Raven from Noah's Ark and why it had to be the Raven that was let out first and then the Dove, how old the Earth really is, along with other Biblical Secrets that theologians and theorists do not know.

I asked, "Is the King James Version of the Word of God the best Word of God we can use today to get the full meaning of the Word of God?" Lay Lay answered, "Yes. The King James Version is the only Real Word of God Bible on the market today. The other versions of the Word of God aren't any good. Some may be close while other Word of God Bibles aren't, but they are actually False Doctrine Bibles. The authors of those False Doctrines actually take out the original meanings and put their own meanings in place of the original meanings that need to be in the Word of God. Just because the book has the title Holy Bible, or some version of the Holy Bible on it doesn't mean it really is the Real

Word of God. I can't stress that enough, human's need to read the King James Version of the Word of God daily. The King James Version is the only Real Word of God Bible on the market today.

The word **'holy'** means <u>**'devoted entirely to the deity or the work of the deity'**</u> **AND 'venerated as OR as if sacred'.** (Merriam Webster)

The word **venerate** means, **'to regard with reverential respect' OR 'with admiring deference' OR 'to honor with a ritual act of devotion'.** (Merriam Webster)

The word **'deity'** means **'the rank or essential nature of A god'** (Notice it says **'a god'**) (Merriam Webster) and **'one exalted or revered as supremely good or powerful'.** (Notice it says, **'revered supremely good OR powerful,** that means **'exalted or revered powerful'** like Satan. He isn't more powerful than Jesus Christ, but he is more powerful than human beings.) (Merriam Webster)

The word **'bible'** means, **'the sacred scriptures of Christians comprising the Old Testament and the New Testament' OR <u>'the sacred scriptures of some other religion'.</u>** (Merriam Webster)

The word **'sacred'** means, **'devoted exclusively to one service' or <u>'worship of a deity'.</u>** (Merriam Webster)

What it all boils down to is 'sacred writings' devoted exclusively to a deity or a god. Jesus Christ has both as well as Satan. The Father in Heaven, Jesus Christ of Nazareth and the Holy Spirit make up the deity. Jesus Christ of Nazareth is only begotten son of the living God, The God Head has a Holy Bible or 'sacred writings'. The Holy Spirit, or Holy Ghost, or Spirit of God which allow the human vessel to see the Spiritual World. Satan is the father, the son is the Anti-Christ, and the holy spirit(s) are the 'Power Demons' or 'Power Unclean Spirits' making up Satan's deity. The Anti-Christ is the son of Satan. Satan has a holy bible or 'sacred writings' known as the Satanist Bible. Power Demons or Power Unclean Spirits allow the human vessel to see the Spiritual World."

Lay Lay continued, "If Detta could get close to the books called the 'Holy Bible', pick them up and actually read some of them with 29 demons running around in her; four of which are Power Demons, then there is no power in those bibles. They are False Doctrine." I asked, "What about all these Church Commentaries, Commentaries from the Bible Bookstores, and Women's Commentaries?" Lay Lay said, "No, commentaries really aren't any good either. They only cover portions of the Word of God. Most of them aren't even using the King James Version of the Word of God for reference. Ask the Holy Spirit to teach you. That's His job and He is very good at teaching the King James Version of the Word of God. Women's Commentaries shouldn't be used. The authors usually use a False Doctrine Holy Bible made by Religious Unclean Spirits to make those, the ones who aren't using False Doctrine are still downplaying the King James Version of the Word of God for women today, changing the words for modern women to be equal to and above man. The authors are trying to please women when they should be pleasing Jesus Christ of Nazareth. Read the King James Version of the Word of God. If any human tries to accept Jesus Christ of Nazareth as their Lord and Savior going by those False Doctrines, Jesus Christ of Nazareth will not accept their Salvation Prayer because it's a Stipulated Prayer. They are actually praying to the Religious Unclean Spirit that changed the words from the King James Version of the Word of God and not to Jesus Christ of Nazareth. If a human had a parent or fiancé overseas and had never seen that parent or fiancé, but that parent wrote several different letters to the child or his fiancée in another language, then that child or fiancée would do everything they could to either learn that language or have someone else translate that language so the child could understand what that parent was talking about. Then that child or fiancée would know the voice of their parent or fiancé and when their parent or fiancé is talking to them by their characteristics. Just like God said to Adam, 'You have listened to the voice of Eve.' Even though Eve didn't say 'Here sweetie, eat this forbidden fruit', she could just as easily have slid the saucer with the apple pie on it in front of Adam and the results would be the same. God gave all His children letters from Him for His children to live by and take to their hearts. God even sent the best 'interpreter' in the universe to help His children with the interpretation of His letters, the Holy Spirit, to teach His children how to read His letters. How is it then, that His children don't know His voice when they hear

Him speaking or His actions? Because they are wanting to do their own thing and when the voice of the Religious Unclean Spirit becomes more dominant in the human mind and heart than the voice of Jesus Christ of Nazareth, the child of Christ can't distinguish between the two voices and gets confused. Eventually they will actually loose their salvation over it just like the Nation of Israel."

SATAN CAN NOT CREATE

I asked, "What about those weird words that man said to me over the phone when Detta was at Satan World Order? What was that? Lay Lay said, "Well, you have heard that Satan has an opposite for everything that God has, right?" I said, "Yes, I've heard that, is it true?" Lay Lay said, "Yes, it's true. Satan can't create anything; all he can do is take what is already created and make it evil. That's what those weird words where. He was using Satanic Tongues the opposite of Tongues of the Holy Spirit from Heaven. He tried to put a Death Wish on you." I said, "It didn't work, did it." Lay Lay laughingly said, "You're still alive aren't you? Whenever a Satanist or someone who uses the power of Satan tries to put a curse on a Christian the curse always bounces off the Christian." I asked, "You mean they don't know it bounces off?" Lay Lay said, "The human is usually stoned all the time so they don't realize the curse bounces off." I asked, "What is Satan's opposite of the Holy Spirit? Lay Lay said, "Power Demons. The Holy Spirit is Omnipresent. That's why Satan needs a lot of Power Demons. They do the same thing the Holy Spirit does only for evil. Power Demons allow a human being to see the Spiritual World. If Jesus Christ wanted you to see the Spiritual World, the Holy Spirit would Prepare the Way and teach you how to see the Spiritual World. Satan uses the Power Demons to allow his servants to see the Spiritual World. Power Demons are called, 'Holy Spirits from Hell'. Since Power Demons aren't Omni-Present, Satan needs a lot of Power Demons to do the same thing the Holy Spirit from Heaven does. That's how Rachael can see me, Shadow, Michael, and Michael's friends when we were fighting the Vampire Unclean Spirits and all the 'ugly things'. Right now Rachael can see the Spiritual World because she is sanctified through you and Jesus Christ is allowing it because of that. Once Detta

Crosses Over, the Holy Spirit from Heaven will be the one that allows her to see the Spiritual World since she is already used to seeing all those things. Remember Rachael was seeing the Spiritual World before Tony ever Crossed Over. Rachael saw Forma manifesting himself when Rachael was six months old because Lillith, the Power Demon was already in her at three months old."

Lay Lay said, "Jesus Christ was and still is perfect. He is the one who created the angels to begin with and the angels through their own Free-Will chose to go with Satan. Satan took God's creation and made them evil or 'unclean'. That's how their names came about to begin with. Devils, demons, 'unclean spirits' etc. All Jesus Christ has to do is actually tell a demon to 'Leave Now' or 'Go' and that demon leaves through fear. A Christian on the other hand, doesn't have the faith Jesus Christ has, nor do they live like Jesus Christ did even when He was on the Earth. Meaning they don't fast and pray as Jesus Christ did on Earth. It's going to take time for the demons to leave the vessel. A demon can stand getting hurt a little if a Christian tries to cast it out. The demon knows if it doesn't make a big scene it will be able to 'trick' a 'fake Christian' (A person who believes they are a Christian, but really are not.) into believing they cast the demon out while the demon is actually still in its home and no one will know the difference. The demons have been doing this, pretty much, ever since Adam and Eve were kicked out of the Garden of Eden. A big factor is, if the Christians are prayed up or not and if the Christians have fasted or not. The reason you can 'Command with Authority' is because of your past. As I said before, 'You don't just take the bull by the horns, you take the bull by the horns and throw that bull to the ground on its back'. You had to rely on Jesus Christ all the time, that taught you in your heart you don't have to put up with the 'crap' of any 'unclean spirit', but a lot of Christians don't have your faith in Jesus Christ. Remember the Apostles coming to Jesus Christ saying, 'We have tried and tried (This tells you the demon didn't leave right away, in fact it tells you the apostles no matter how hard they tried, couldn't get that demon to leave the vessel.), but this demon will not come out of this person.' Jesus Christ said, 'Oh, ye of little faith.' Then Jesus Christ continued, making this a very big point, 'This type', meaning there are several different types of demons, Jesus Christ doesn't have to talk to the demons to find out what type they are like you do. He created them. He already knows what type the demon is, 'of demon only comes out with prayer and fasting' (Saying the amount of hurting the demon is able to withstand and still not come out of the vessel. The Apostles were using the name of Jesus Christ to try to cast the demon into Hell, it still wasn't leaving.). See the apostles tried and tried to get that demon out of that vessel with no success. Each demon is different. Not all demons leave the vessel as fast as others do."

I asked, "What about the scripture about the people going to Jesus Christ and saying, "'Lord I cast out demons in your name' and Jesus Christ says 'depart from me, I know you not'." Lay Lay said, "Just because a human believes it's a demon doesn't mean it really is. Notice, Jesus Christ didn't say the human cast the demon out in His name, the human did. There was one example that a human was praying and a little spit came out of their mouth. Another human said, "That must be a demon, 'I command you to go to Hell in the name of Jesus'. Then the human believed they actually cast a demon into Hell and started saying, 'Thank you Jesus, Oh, and Glory'. That human didn't cast a demon to Hell, he told a little spit to go to Hell. That particular human didn't have the power to cast a demon to Hell. He wasn't saved himself, he was gay and he had a Religious Unclean Spirit in him. He had at least two demons in him, one for being 'gay' and one for 'teaching the Religious False Doctrine from Satan' and with those particular types of demons it would be considered a 'Legion of Unclean Spirits'. Remember, a 'Legion' of 'unclean spirits' is two or more depending on the type and power of each 'unclean spirit'. He said the Sinners Prayer, from a 'False Doctrine Bible' that a Religious Unclean Spirit made that is on the market, so Jesus Christ of Nazareth didn't come in. He was singing songs about Jesus in church, using the name of Jesus in the songs. Just because a person sings songs about Jesus in church services and acts the act, doesn't mean they are saved, he never did say the whole name of Jesus Christ of Nazareth. One of those masks that humans wear and no one knows. A real demon could have torn that human to shreds or entered that vessel and the human wouldn't have known anything about it. He was 'walking the walk' and 'talking the talk' according to everyone that knew him."

I ask, "How long does it take for Christians to pray a demon out of a vessel? Or healing for a Christian?" Lay Lay said, "That's a big misconception that Christians have when they read the Word of God today. Christians only read a certain passage and believe they know from that passage alone. Humans are so used to things happening 'right now', 'instantly', that they think a few seconds of prayer will do the job. It may take several minutes to several hours to get a demon to leave a vessel. It will take several hours to get the demons out of this vessel. Yes, Jesus Christ did order the demons out and most of the time they immediately left. How many Christians live like Jesus Christ did? How many spend hours a day praying and fasting like Jesus Christ did? You can't get a job done without the proper training and readiness. Other times 'unclean spirits' didn't leave immediately, like the story of Legion and the explanation of Matthew's word 'two' Jesus Christ pointed out to you because of Detta's mind being split and Tony and Mandy being in her vessel as well. The Apostles had big fights on their hands. Look at it this way. You are living in your home for years and then someone wants to come along and make you leave without you wanting to leave. Now you are going to put up a big fight, even to the extent of getting hurt, before you leave won't you? We aren't talking about Court Papers making someone move without putting up a fight here. Back in the old days even a century ago there was no such thing as an Eviction Notice or a Restraining Order. Just because times have changed for these things to happen in the Physical World, doesn't mean they have changed that way in the Spiritual World. That demon in the vessel is going to put up a big fight even with Christians praying and using the name of Jesus Christ and Pleading the Blood of Christ and the Cross of Calvary. Yes, the demon will shudder, the demon will get hurt by the name of Jesus Christ being used all the time and Pleading the Blood, but the Power Demons are used to that. The Power Demons are the ones who are sent to people who have had demons cast out and don't really accept Christ in their hearts. The human saying the words think that does the job like Tony did.

Matthew 12:43-45 (KJV)

43) 'When the unclean spirit is gone out (commanded to leave) of the man, he (The male or female unclean spirit. He is masculine for either sex like a lot of the foreign languages use today when talking about a male and female possibility.) walketh through dry places, seeking rest (the unclean spirits need a vessel to rest in), and findeth none.'

44) 'Then he saith, I will return into my house from whence I came out; and when he is come, he findeth it (the vessel) empty, swept, and garnished (clean, ready to live in).'

45) 'Then goeth he, and taketh with himself seven other spirits more wicked than himself, and they enter in and dwell there: and the last state of that man is worse than the first. Even so shall it be also unto this wicked generation.' The demon will leave a for a season and come back to the vessel and if the demon finds the vessel clean like a brand new house never lived in before and all decorated up just like out of the factory, the mother's womb (Meaning Jesus Christ is not living in the vessel), the unclean spirit will go and get seven others stronger than himself and return to the vessel to live in it. The vessel will be even worse off than before. What Christians forget is the demon is really an 'unclean spirit'."

Luke. 11:25 (KJV)

25) And when he cometh, he findeth *it* swept and garnished.

Lay Lay continued, "In human terms, when the 'unclean spirit' leaves the vessel it's like taking soap and water to clean the vessel. In human terms, if the 'unclean spirit' leaves the vessel on its own like in 'legion' where the 'unclean spirits' came and went when they chose to, or if a Christian casts the demons to Hell and the human being doesn't really accept Christ, then the vessel is still considered to be 'clean'. Where humans get confused is when they think since they are born into sin, that means the heart of the vessel is dirty from birth. That's not the case; being born into sin simply means the soul and spirit can't get into Heaven without the Blood of Christ. The shell is going to sin because the vessel is born into sin. The heart is still empty, swept (clean), and garnished when the vessel is born. The heart stays empty, swept (clean), and garnished until either an 'unclean spirit' or the Holy Spirit and Jesus Christ go into the vessel." I asked, "What is Lillith's true form anyway?" Lay Lay laughed and said, "You wouldn't like it. Her true form is a 'snake'." I said, "That's why I keep hearing a 'hissing' sound when I talk to her. It's her snake tongue making that 'hissing' sound. It must be huge, it sounds like the 'purr' of a huge lion." Lay Lay said, "Yes, Shadow and I are still trying to figure out a way out for you not to have sex with Lillith." I asked, "Why is that?" Lay Lay said, "Because in the Spiritual World your words are a 'contract'." I said, "Yes, I realized that after the first time, when the demon tried to bribe me. That's why, with Lillith, I never did say I wanted to have sex with her to begin with. I always put it in the form of a question. Asking her how much she wanted to have sex with me. I was very careful about that." I asked, "Would you mind doing me a favor if Jesus Christ allows it?" Lay Lay asked, "What's that?" I said, "Well, we have been through a lot together, it would be nice if you could meet me at the Pearly Gates when I get to Heaven. It would be nice to be able to meet you face to face." Lay Lay hesitated for a second and said, "I believe that can be arranged."

JACOB

AND

JOSEPH

(CONTINUED FROM: HEAVENLY ANGEL LAY LAY EXPLAINS THE DIFFERENCE BETWEEN A 'COLD CHRISTIAN' AND A 'BACKSLIDER')

After I tell the reader Biblical Facts that Heavenly Angel Lay Lay told me when I was working with her and Shadow, I will be writing about different stories from the King James Version of the Word of God talking about the family aspects in the Word of God. How the different couples in the bible met, what the couples went through, and what men, women, and children are commanded to do and not to do according to the Word of God. Just like HEAVENLY ANGEL LAY LAY taught me how to do.

JACOB AND JOSEPH

Genesis 35:1-29
1) And God said unto Jacob, Arise, go up to Bethel, and dwell there: and make there an altar unto God, that appeared unto thee when thou fleddest from the face of Esau thy brother. (Now from **Shechem to Bethel** is 20 miles or 30 kilometers south. Traveling 25 miles or 41.75 kilometers a day by camel it would take less than a day to travel) (1.67 kilometers per mile so 25 miles x1.67=41.75 kilometers) (Merriam-Webster)
2) Then Jacob said unto his household, and to all that were with him, Put away the strange gods (back into idol worshipping) that are among you, and be clean, and change your garments: (Now this is important, when Jacob said get rid of all the 'false gods', he not only said that to his own household, but to everyone that were in his care)
3) And let us arise, and go up to Bethel; and I will make there an altar unto God, who answered me in the day of my distress, and was with me in the way which I went.
4) And they gave unto Jacob all the strange gods which were in their hand, and all their earrings which were in their ears; and Jacob hid them under the oak which was by Shechem. (They are still in Shechem, Jacob is getting rid of all the idols before they

leave Shechem)

5) And they journeyed: and the terror of God was upon the cities that were round about them, and they did not pursue after the sons of Jacob.

6) So Jacob came to Luz, which is in the land of Canaan, that is, Bethel, he and all the people that were with him. (A new start with no 'false gods')

7) And he built there an altar, and called the place Elbethel: because there God appeared unto him, when he fled from the face of his brother.

8) But Deborah Rebekah's nurse died, and she was buried beneath Bethel under an oak: and the name of it was called Allonbachuth.

9) And God appeared unto Jacob again, when he came out of Padanaram, and blessed him.

10) And God said unto him, **Thy name is Jacob: thy name shall not be called any more Jacob, but Israel shall be thy name: and he called his name Israel.**

11) And God said unto him, I am God Almighty: be fruitful and multiply; a nation and a company of nations shall be of thee, and kings shall come out of thy loins;

12) And the land which I gave Abraham and Isaac, to thee I will give it, and to thy seed after thee will I give the land.

13) And God went up from him (Jacob) in the place where he (God) talked with him (Jacob).

14) **And Jacob set up a pillar in the place where he (God) talked with him (Jacob), even a pillar of stone: and he (Jacob) poured a drink offering thereon, and he (Jacob) poured oil (anointed) thereon. (Here is an excellent example of us being able to anoint an inanimate object, a stone as this case, or a building, etc.** More about this in my book MATTHEW'S WORD 'TWO':REAL WORD OF GOD BIBLE)

15) And Jacob called the name of the place where God spake with him, Bethel.

16) And they journeyed from Bethel; and there was but a little way to come to Ephrath: and Rachel travailed, and she (Rachel) had hard labour. (15 miles or 25.05 kilometers south. 15 miles x

1.67 = 25.05/25 miles per day travel by camel= 0.6 days travel)

17) And it came to pass, when she (Rachel) was in hard labour, that the midwife (Now remember, Rachel's other midwife or nurse, Deborah, the one with all the experience in child bearing, had died already. This was a new midwife) said unto her, Fear not; thou shalt have this son also.

18) And it came to pass (During a long labor), as her (Rachel's) soul was in departing (How many women would do this now days? If there are any complications at all, the mother can have the child killed in order to same the mother's life and the father won't even know about the murder of the unborn child. **A mother is to give her life for the life of her child, unborn or born. Rachel gave her life for Benjamin and Benjamin plays a very important role in a lot of future events when it comes to Joseph, the Israelites, Egypt, Jacob going to Egypt after Benjamin, and all that leads right into Moses and Canaan Land again. If Rachel would have been stingy like women in the United States today, Benjamin would have been aborted in order to same Rachel's life and Jacob would never have seen Joseph again after Joseph's brothers sold him as a slave because Jacob never would have made the trip into Egypt to retrieve Benjamin. If that wouldn't have happened, then the Israelites never would have gone into Egypt to begin with and all would have perished for lack of food. Rachel had no idea how important Benjamin was going to play in all the future events)**, (for she died) that she (Rachel) called his (the child's) name Benoni: but his (the child's) father (Jacob) called him (the child) Benjamin.

19) And Rachel died, and was buried in the way to Ephrath, which is Bethlehem. (Rachel died during child birth to Benjamin)

20) And Jacob set a pillar upon her grave: that is the pillar of Rachel's grave unto this day. (Rachel's grave is still marked)

21) And Israel (Israel is Jacob, remember? God changed Jacob's name to Israel after Jacob wrestled with the angel and won) journeyed, and spread his tent beyond the tower of Edar.

22) And it came to pass, when Israel dwelt in that land, that

Reuben went and lay (had sex) with Bilhah his father's concubine (Rachel's handmade, one of Jacob/Israel's wives): and Israel heard it. Now the sons of Jacob were twelve: (We need to go back to Noah for a minute for an explanation of what's going on)

Genesis 9:20-25

20) And Noah began to be an husbandman, and he planted a vineyard:

21) And he (Noah and his wife) drank of the wine, and was **drunken** (This is past the stage of Driving While Intoxicated, not a mere Driving Under the Influence of Intoxicants); **and he (Noah) was uncovered within his tent** (Noah went in his tent and passed out. When a person passes out from alcohol intake, if they do take the time to undress, which a lot of them don't. They always cover up, their body temperature is lower than normal due to the alcohol in the blood system, no matter what the outside temperature is, they will always feel cold and cover up. They may wake up later in a daze and throw the covers off, but they always cover up when they first go to bed and 'pass out'. Not only that, but **their custom was to sleep in their clothes to begin with, so Noah had his clothes on when he 'passed out'.** This rules out Ham just seeing Noah naked in bed. The word 'he', is talking about Noah's wife. They were 'one flesh'. Ham took advantage of Noah's wife, Ham's mother, having had alcohol that night as well as Noah).

22) And **Ham**, the father of Canaan, **saw the nakedness of his father (Ham had sex with Noah's wife, Ham's mother, while Noah was passed out in his tent**), and told his two brethren without (Ham bragged to his two brothers outside the tent about having sex with Noah's wife, Ham's mother, after his two brothers had come around the tent area, while Noah was still 'passed out' from drinking, 'without' means 'outside the tent'. Some think the 'nakedness' means Noah was broke, but at that time, Noah was very wealthy. He and his family were the only ones that made it past the 'great flood'. Noah had everything on Earth, he couldn't have been broke. The scripture says 'Noah awoke', this rules out Noah 'blacking out'. When a person 'blacks out' they don't remember anything. It also couldn't mean

that Ham saw Noah naked and sleeping off the alcohol because if that's what happened there would be no evidence of Ham even going into the tent to begin with and the scriptures say that 'Noah awoke from his wine', also Noah would still have on his undergarments. No tent flap opening is going to wake anyone up if they are 'passed out' from alcohol. The person would have to 'sleep it off' before they wake up. Nakedness in this case couldn't mean that Ham had sex with Noah either, because if Ham had raped Noah, Noah would have been more awake immediately instead of in a daze and wouldn't have waited to curse Ham instead of waiting until the next day. The only alternative left is that Ham had sex with Ham's mother, Noah's wife. I had to put two scriptures from Leviticus 18 in here for everyone to understand it because they are directly tied into these verses for clarity. In verse 24 it specifically states that **'Noah awoke from his wine'**, meaning Noah had 'passed out' and not 'blacked out' before Ham ever went into the tent)

Leviticus 18:6-8

6) None of you shall approach to any that is near of kin to him, **to uncover their nakedness**: I am the LORD.

7) **The nakedness of thy father, or the nakedness of thy mother, shalt thou not uncover** (The word 'uncover' means . A lot of countries have different cultures, but the Word of God is for everyone. Some cultures allow their women to run around topless while their legs are totally covered, some cultures cover both top and legs, some cultures cover only the top and not the legs, but all the cultures that I know of cover the woman's vaginal area. 'Uncover' means to separate the females, I use the word 'female' here because a little girl is not a woman yet, vaginal lips uncovering her vagina and clitoris for touching, licking, sucking, or penetration of any kind. On a male it would include touching or sucking on the genitalia, scrotums, penis, head, etc. Changing some ones diaper or cleaning them up after they poop or pee their diapers or pants are not considered 'uncovering their nakedness', that's why the 'hymen' of the girl is far enough inside her to allow for cleanups and still be in tact and the Israelites had to be circumcised to take the 'foreskin' off

the boys, get it? Nursing Assistants, and in their times, the person could have been called a 'Midwife' clean up a patient if the patient can not control their bodily functions. The person uncontrollably poops and pees their pants and need to be cleaned and changed. That's not 'seeing someone's nakedness'. There is no sexual intent or desire for sexual intent to changing some ones diaper or clothes and cleaning up their mess if they can not do that themselves. God knew what He was doing when He created us): she is thy mother; thou shalt not uncover her nakedness.

8) **THE NAKEDNESS OF THY FATHER'S WIFE shalt thou not uncover: IT IS THY FATHER'S NAKEDNESS.**

23) And Shem and Japheth took a garment, and laid it upon both their shoulders, **and went backward**, and covered the nakedness of their father; (Noah's wife had her clothes on until Ham went in and laid with her, then, 'Noah's nakedness was uncovered', she had no clothes on because Ham had just had sex with her) and their faces were backward (Shem and Japheth made sure their faces were not able to see their naked mother when they backed into the tent), and they saw not their father's nakedness (They never saw their naked mother. When Shem and Japheth took the garment in they went in BACKWARDS so they wouldn't see their naked mother. The father and mother are 'one flesh', you intentionally see the 'private part' or 'have sex' with the 'wife' of the man, you have seen the 'nakedness of the man'. If you don't believe this, think about all the Venereal Diseases that are spread that way. The husband or wife get it first, then spread it to their spouse. They are 'one flesh')

24) And <u>Noah awoke from his wine</u>, **and knew what his younger son had done unto him**. [Noah had already passed out before Ham went into the tent and had sex with Noah's wife. **'and knew what his younger son had done unto him'** tells us there was some time that had passed from the time Ham was in the tent and the time that Noah woke from his wine. Ham had already left the tent again before Noah woke from his wine. **'Noah awoke from his wine'**. This also tells me Noah's body was used to the alcohol because if he wasn't used to the alcohol,

Noah would have gotten sick and vomited the alcohol up instead of just passing out unable to do anything. Noah had too much to drink like Lot did when Lot's daughters raped Lot. Lot's daughters cleaned up the mess where Noah saw the evidence. A 'totally naked' wife beside Noah who is only covered with a sheet or bedspread because Shem and Japheth laid it over her and a 'wet spot' in the middle of the sheets she is laying on is a sure sign of sexual intercourse. Noah lived in a time that was worse than Lot, Ham was used to seeing abominations like sons having sex with mothers, throughout the Earth (Demonic Oppression, the demon attaching to the vessel or Demonic Possession, the demon actually living in the vessel) before the 'Great Flood', that's why God flooded the earth to begin with. Noah's body was used to the alcohol content just like Lot's, meaning Noah was an alcoholic as well as Lot and they were both just and upright men in the eyes of God. **Noah and Lot were both suffering from depression.** If you don't think their Blood Alcohol Content was over a .08 you're kidding yourself, now days in some states the BAC only has to be .04. Several years ago there was no such thing as a BAC, so Noah and Lot's BAC was far above any legal limit we have now days. People have a pre-conceived idea that an alcoholic has to be a 'bum' living out of a bottle of whiskey in a street alley, that's not true. I know alcoholics who work hard every day, come home, clean up, eat, and then go out again all night drinking and 'having fun'. How do I know an alcoholic can do that? I used to do that myself, except my 'having fun' was 'playing pool' instead of 'having sex' with some other man's wife or girlfriend. Some of them were into drugs, some weren't. Drugs certainly don't help in the process. I never did get into the drug scene, that's why I never really did fit in with a lot of the women. If a person has to drink or do drugs to 'have fun', they aren't in their right minds when they 'have fun' to begin with. That tells me they are not capable of 'having fun' when they are in their right minds. I drank so much because of loosing my first son during a divorce after my ex had an affair with a salesman and my second ex having an orgy with a man and woman and getting my other two boys in the custody battle after she married a Convicted Child Molester. I didn't want to think about what my own boys were possibly having done to them and there was nothing I could do about it, it's impossible to get evidence when the custodial parent is always told if the non-custodial parent ever wants any information about their own children, even if that reason is to protect the children. Her parents were Foster Care Parents and had connections in the county. Not only the Foster Program, but also the Child Protection Program and the Police in Umatilla County Oregon. All this and more will be in another book I'm going to title, 'What's Wrong With This Picture?' At the time of this copyright, I will be 'alcohol free' for two years now, my sobriety date is June 27, 2004. Anyway, Noah and Lot both put God first, but still drank to get some relief from the pain and anger in their hearts due to the cultures they lived in. If you think building the ark, possibly for years, with a bright blue, sunny, hot, sky over your head while people were mocking your every move day after day wasn't stressful, you are kidding yourself. You see the difference between Noah and Lot. The whole story of Lot is in my book MATTHEW'S WORD 'TWO': REAL WORD OF GOD BIBLE. For this book let's just say that I was helping Rachel out of Satanism. Satan didn't give her soul up without a fight. When Satan threw spiritual things at us, Jesus countered those Spiritual Fights with backup of three different Heavenly Angels. Heavenly Angle Lay Lay is one of the three different Heavenly Angel I was allowed to talk to and work with when I was helping Rachel out of Satanism. This is just a portion of the story about Lot. Just like Heavenly Angel Lay Lay said, 'Look at the characteristics, not the titles.' And, 'Christians today don't need to feel they are so far below the Prophets and Apostles they can't get to the level of the Prophets and Apostles, the Prophets and Apostles were human too. The Prophets and Apostles made mistakes just like Christians today.' The more I search the scriptures and look at the characteristics instead of the titles. The more I find they had a lot of difficulties and were weak in 'faith' just like we are today, but God still used each and every one of them in Powerful Ways]

Talking about Lot and his two virgin daughters:
Genesis 19:31-38

31) And the firstborn said unto the younger, Our father is old, and there is not a man in the earth to come in unto us after the manner of all the earth:

32) Come, let us make our father drink wine, and we will lie with him, that we may preserve seed of our father.

33) And they made their father drink wine that night: and the firstborn went in, and lay with her father; **and he perceived not when she lay down, nor when she arose**. (See, they are the same, only Noah knew by the evidence where Lot's daughters cleaned up the evidence. Noah didn't know either until he woke up from his wine, then he saw the evidence where Lot didn't have any evidence to see because his daughters cleaned the evidence up after they were done)

34) And it came to pass on the morrow, that the firstborn said unto the younger, Behold, I lay yesternight with my father: let us make him drink wine this night also; and go thou in, and lie with him, that we may preserve seed of our father.

35) And they made their father drink wine that night also: and the younger arose, and lay with him; **and he perceived not when she lay down, nor when she arose**. (Here is the difference again between Noah and Lot)

36) Thus were both the daughters of Lot with child by their father.

37) And the first born bare a son, and called his name Moab: the same is the father of the Moabites unto this day.

38) And the younger, she also bare a son, and called his name Benammi: the same is the father of the children of Ammon unto this day.

Back to Noah:

25) **And he (Noah) said, Cursed be Canaan** (Noah was extremely angry with Ham and cursed Ham through Canaan, Ham's youngest son. See it's not a sin for a Christian to be angry, it's actually good for the human to get angry and release that anger, even Jesus got angry. If you think Noah didn't

scream and yell at Ham while Noah was cursing Ham you're kidding yourself again); a servant of servants shall he be unto his brethren. (The three to four generation curse went into effect when Ham had sex with his mother. Why the son of Ham? Because Noah didn't want Ham to teach Canaan to do the abominable act that Ham did to Noah's wife, if it wasn't too late already. Canaan, already knowing how to do abominations, had to be lower than the brothers and Canaan had to be a servant to the others in hopes that the others would help straighten Canaan out if it wasn't already too late. The servant always has to listen to, obey, and learn from their master. In today's terms, Ham was 'unfit' to be a father to Canaan so Noah 'placed' Canaan with his relatives, not with someone outside the family. In today's terms, Canaan was given to 'blood relatives' and not put in 'Foster Care'. Ham's older sons were already of age and out of the house)

Now back to Jacob and Rachel:

23) The sons of Leah; Reuben, Jacob's firstborn, and Simeon, and Levi, and Judah, and Issachar, and Zebulun:

24) The sons of Rachel; Joseph, and Benjamin:

25) And the sons of Bilhah, Rachel's handmaid; Dan, and Naphtali:

26) And the sons of Zilpah, Leah's handmaid: Gad, and Asher: these are the sons of Jacob, which were born to him in Padanaram.

27) And **Jacob came unto Isaac his father unto Mamre, unto the city of Arbah, which is Hebron, where Abraham and Isaac sojourned (temporarily stayed)**.

28) And the days of Isaac were an hundred and fourscore (180) years.

29) And Isaac gave up the ghost (his spirit left his body), and died (his body died), and was gathered unto his people, being old and full of days: and his sons Esau and Jacob buried him. (Now Jacob is in Hebron)

GENESIS 37:1-36

1) And Jacob dwelt in the land wherein his father was a stranger, in the land of Canaan. (Hebron)

2) These are the generations of Jacob. **Joseph, being seventeen years old**, was feeding the flock with his brethren; and the lad was with the sons of Bilhah, and with the sons of Zilpah, his father's wives: and Joseph brought unto his father their evil report. (Joseph tattled on his brothers about their bad deeds)

3) Now Israel (Remember Jacob received the name of Israel after he wrestled with an angel all night and won. Jacob had to have been a huge man) loved Joseph more than all his children (Remember, Joseph was the youngest son of Rachel before they left Rachel's homeland where Jacob and Rachel were married), because he (Joseph) was the son of his (Jacob's) old age: and he (Jacob) made him (Joseph) a coat of many colours.

4) And when his (Joseph's) brethren (brothers) saw that their father (Jacob/Israel) loved him (Joseph) more than all his brethren, they (Joseph's brothers) hated him (Joseph), and could not speak peaceably unto him. (Joseph's brothers were always hateful toward Joseph)

5) And Joseph dreamed a dream, and he (Joseph) told it (the dream) his brethren: and they (Joseph's brothers) hated him (Joseph) yet the more. (Even more than they did before)

6) And he (Joseph) said unto them (his brothers), Hear, I pray you, this dream which I have dreamed:

7) For, behold, we were binding sheaves in the field, and, lo, my sheaf arose, and also stood upright; and, behold, your sheaves stood round about, and made obeisance (bowed down, respected) to my sheaf.

8) And his brethren said to him (Joseph), Shalt thou indeed reign over us? or shalt thou indeed have dominion over us? And they hated him yet the more for his dreams, and for his words. (Now Joseph's brothers really hated Joseph)

9) And he (Joseph) dreamed yet another dream, and told it his brethren, and said, Behold, I have dreamed a dream more (again); and, behold, the sun and the moon and the eleven stars made obeisance (bowed down, respected) to me (Joseph).

10) And he told it (the dream) to his father, and to his brethren:

and his father rebuked (told Joseph he was wrong) him, and said unto him (Joseph), What is this dream that thou hast dreamed? Shall I and thy mother and thy brethren indeed come to bow down ourselves to thee to the earth?

11) And his brethren envied him; but his father observed the saying.

12) And his brethren (Joseph's brothers) went to feed their father's flock in Shechem.   (Joseph goes from Hebron to Shechem which is 80 miles or 133.6 kilometers north)

13) And Israel said unto Joseph, Do not thy brethren feed the flock in Shechem? come, and I will send thee unto them. And he (Joseph) said to him (Israel), Here am I.

14) And he (Israel) said to him (Joseph), Go, I pray thee, see whether it be well with thy brethren, and well with the flocks; and bring me word again (Let me know if everything is well with your brothers and the flocks). So he (Israel) sent him (Joseph) out of the vale of Hebron, and he (Joseph) came to Shechem.

15) And a certain man found him (Joseph), and, behold, he (Joseph) was wandering in the field: and the man asked him (Joseph), saying, What seekest thou?

16) And he (Joseph) said, I seek my brethren: tell me, I pray thee, where they (Joseph's brothers) feed their flocks.

17) And the man said, They are departed hence (Joseph's brothers already left Shechem); for I heard them say, Let us go to Dothan. And Joseph went after his brethren, and found them in Dothan.   (Shechem to Dothan is about 15 miles or 25.05 kilometers north. Less than a day's journey. 25 miles per day or 42.50 kilometers per day travel by camel)

18) And when they (Joseph's brothers) saw him (Joseph) afar off, even before he (Joseph) came near unto them (Joseph's brothers), they (Joseph's brothers) conspired against him (Joseph) to slay (Kill) him (Joseph).

19) And they said one to another, Behold, this dreamer cometh (Referring to Joseph).

20) Come now therefore, and let us slay him (Joseph), and cast him (Joseph) into some pit, and we will say, Some evil beast hath devoured him (Joseph): and we shall see what will become of his

dreams (Jealousy, hatred, anger).

21) And Reuben heard it, and he (Reuben, Leah's first born to Israel) delivered him (Joseph) out of their hands; and said, Let us not kill him.

22) And Reuben said unto them, Shed no blood, but cast him (Joseph) into this pit that is in the wilderness, and lay no hand upon him; that he might rid him out of their hands, to deliver him to his father again (Reuben was planning on keeping Joseph safe until the other brothers were gone and then help Joseph get back to their father, Israel again).

23) And it came to pass, when Joseph was come unto his brethren, that they stript (forcefully took) Joseph out of his coat, his coat of many colours that was on him (that coat was made by Jacob, Joseph's father especially for Joseph, remember? To this day, even in the secular world, that coat of many colors is not only remembered, but also recognized for its love of a father to his son. A lot of moms use several pieces of cloth and stitch, and sew them together to make clothing for their children with love in every stitch. No manufacturing company could ever out do any article of clothing made with pieces of cloth and love in every stitch);

24) And they (Joseph's brothers) took him (Joseph), and cast him (Joseph) into a pit: and the pit was empty, there was no water in it. (It must have been an old abandoned well or hole that never struck water when they were digging for a well)

25) And they (Joseph's brothers) sat down to eat bread: and they lifted up their eyes and looked, and, behold, a company of Ishmeelites came from Gilead with their camels bearing spicery and balm and myrrh, going to carry it down to Egypt. (This is interesting, the Ishmeelites came from Gilead, Gilead is south east of Dothan just above and on the east side of the Dead Sea. In other words, the Ishmeelites had to travel north west to Dothan, then backtrack south to Egypt, also going right through Hebron where Joseph's father, Jacob AKA Israel was living. Also remember that Ishmael is the founder of the Ishmeelites and Ishmael was the 'bastard child' of Abraham and Hagar, Sarah's handmaid. Ishmael lived in the Wilderness of Paran just North of

Egypt where Hagar was from. Also remember that Hagar was the daughter of the Pharaoh of the king of Egypt at the time Hagar was given to Sarai. Ishmael was also 'possessed after Hagar chose a wife for Ishmael from Egypt, 'idol worshippers'. Ishmael lived as a 'wild man' in the Wilderness of Paran. Ishmael was the brother of Isaac, Isaac was Joseph's grandfather) 26) And Judah (A wicked brother of Joseph's. We will see just how wicked in the next chapter) said unto his brethren, What profit is it if we slay our brother, and conceal his blood?

27) Come, and let us (the brothers) sell him (Joseph) to the Ishmeelites, and let not our hand be upon him; for he is our brother and our flesh. And his brethren were content. (We will see in verse 29 that Reuben was not around when Joseph's brothers planned all this)

28) Then there passed by Midianites merchantmen; and they (the brothers) drew and lifted up Joseph out of the pit, and sold Joseph to the Ishmeelites for twenty pieces of silver: and they (the merchantmen) brought Joseph into Egypt. (Joseph went right through Hebron where Israel, Joseph's father was, right through the Desert Shur which is just east of the Wilderness of Paran where the descendants of Ishmael, Joseph's grandfather's brother settled down at, right into Egypt where Hagar the princess of Egypt, Sarai's handmaid, was from)

29) And Reuben returned (Reuben wasn't around when Judah talked the other brothers into selling Joseph into slavery) unto the pit; and, behold, Joseph was not in the pit; and he (Reuben) rent (tore) his clothes.

30) And he (Reuben) returned unto his brethren, and said, The child (Joseph) is not; and I, whither shall I go?

31) And they (Joseph's brothers) took Joseph's coat, and killed a kid of the goats, and dipped the coat in the blood;

32) And they (Joseph's brothers) sent the coat of many colours, and they (Joseph's brothers) brought it to their father (Jacob); and said, This have we found: know now whether it be thy son's coat or no.

33) And he (Israel) knew it, and said, It is my son's coat; an evil beast hath devoured (eaten) him; Joseph is without doubt rent

(torn) in pieces.

34) And Jacob (Israel) rent (tore) his clothes, and put sackcloth upon his loins, and mourned for his son many days.

35) And all his sons (Joseph's brothers) and all his daughters (Joseph's sisters. This is the first time we even know Joseph had any sisters except Dinah, remember the daughter of Leah who laid with the prince and the prince wanted to make Dinah his wife and a Princess of his father's land before Dinah's brothers killed all the men of that land and Jacob had to order everyone out of that land? This happened when Joseph was between an infant and a lad, long before Benjamin came along) rose up to comfort him (Jacob); but he (Jacob) refused to be comforted; and he (Jacob) said, For I will go down into the grave unto my son mourning. Thus his (Joseph's) father (Jacob) wept for him (Joseph).

36) And the Midianites sold him (Joseph) into Egypt unto Potiphar, an officer of Pharaoh's, and captain of the guard.

GENESIS 38:1-30

1) And it came to pass at that time, that Judah (one of Joseph's brothers, a son of Leah) went down from (left) his brethren, and turned in to a certain Adullamite, whose name was Hirah.

2) And Judah saw there a daughter of a certain Canaanite, whose name was Shuah; and he took her, and went in unto her. (Now remember, no offspring of Noah's or Abraham's were to go outside the 'Proper Physical Bloodline'. A son was NOT to take a wife from the Canaanites, but to go to Haran where their family tree originated from for their wives in order to keep the 'Proper Physical Bloodline' clean. The 'Proper Physical Bloodline' is explained in detail in my book MATTHEW'S WORD 'TWO':REAL WORD OF GOD BIBLE by Heavenly Angel Lay Lay. Marrying a woman outside the 'Proper Physical Bloodline' was one of Judah's huge mistakes)

3) And she (Shuah) conceived, and bare a son; and he (Judah) called his (the child's) name Er.

4) And she (Shuah) conceived again, and bare a son; and she (this time Shuah, the mother named the child which is totally against

the Order of Creation, not to mention the Order of Husband and Wife. Anything against the Order of Creation is from Satan) called his name Onan.

5) And she (Shuah) yet again conceived, and bare a son; and called his name Shelah (again, going against the Order of Creation and the Order of the Husband and Wife): and he (Judah) was at Chezib, when she (Shuah) bare him (the child).

6) And Judah took a wife for Er his firstborn, whose name was Tamar.

7) And Er, Judah's firstborn, was wicked in the sight of the Lord; and the Lord slew him.

8) And Judah said unto Onan, Go in unto thy brother's wife, and marry her, and raise up seed to thy brother.

9) And Onan knew that the seed should not be his (this is Onan's own Free-Will, that is talked about in dept in my book MATTHEW'S WORD 'TWO':REAL WORD OF GOD BIBLE); and it came to pass, when he went in unto his brother's wife, that he spilled it on the ground (Onan allowed his sperm to go on the ground), lest that he should give seed to his brother. (Onan didn't want to give his dead brother a child. Onan is leaning on his own understanding and not by the Word of God)

10) And the thing (Onan allowing his sperm to go to a place other than where the man's sperm was created to do) which he (Onan) did displeased the Lord: wherefore he (God) slew (killed) him (Onan) also. (Here is a perfect example of whether or not it's a sin for a male or female to 'masturbate', I use the terms 'male or female' because a boy or girl could 'masturbate' as well. Masturbation is an abomination. Masturbation is worse than 'lust' and 'adultery'. Onan taking Tamar as his wife wasn't either lust or adultery so God wouldn't have killed Onan if Onan had gotten Tamar pregnant, but Onan refused, so God killed Onan also).

11) Then said Judah to Tamar his daughter in law, Remain a widow at thy father's house (now here is where a widow is to go if her father is still alive. In other words, a widow or widower is to go back to their family, either the father, mother, brother, sister, etc), till Shelah my son be grown: for he (Judah) said, Lest

peradventure he (Shelah) die also, as his brethren did. And Tamar went and dwelt in her father's house. (Tamar waited for Shelah, Judah's youngest son to become of age for marriage to take her to wife)

12) And in process of time the daughter of Shuah Judah's wife died; and Judah was comforted, and went up unto his sheepshearers to Timnath, he and his friend Hirah the Adullamite.

13) And it was told Tamar, saying, Behold thy father in law goeth up to Timnath to shear his sheep.

14) And she (Tamar) put her widow's garments off from her, and covered her with a vail, and wrapped herself, and sat in an open place, which is by the way to Timnath; for she saw that Shelah (Judah's youngest son) was grown, and she (Tamar) was not given unto him (Shelah) to wife.

15) When Judah saw her (Tamar), he (Judah) thought her (Tamar) to be an harlot; because she (Tamar) had covered her face.

16) And he (Judah) turned unto her (Tamar) by the way, and said, Go to, I pray thee, let me come in unto thee; (for he knew not that she was his daughter in law.) And she said, What wilt thou give me, that thou mayest come in unto me? (Tamar is playing a harlot, wanting money or merchandise for sex)

17) And he (Judah) said, I will send thee (you) a kid from the flock. And she (Tamar) said, Wilt thou give me a pledge, till thou send it?

18) And he (Judah) said, What pledge shall I give thee? And she (Tamar) said, Thy signet, and thy bracelets, and thy staff that is in thine (your) hand. And he (Judah) gave it her (Tamar), and came in unto her (Tamar), and she (Tamar) conceived by him (Judah). (Now we have a daughter in law who conspired to lay with her father in law and conceived a child by her father in law. This is really bad and a definite abomination)

19) And she (Tamar) arose, and went away, and laid by her vail from her, and put on the garments of her widowhood. (Tamar has gone back to dressing like a widow again)

20) And Judah sent the kid by the hand of his friend the

Adullamite, to receive his pledge from the woman's hand: but he (the Adullamite) found her (Tamar) not.

21) Then he (the Adullamite) asked the men of that place, saying, Where is the harlot, that was openly by the way side? And they (the men of that place) said, There was no harlot in this place.

22) And he (the Adullamite) returned to Judah, and said, I cannot find her (the harlot); and also the men of the place said, that there was no harlot in this place.

23) And Judah said, Let her (the harlot) take it (the articles that Judah gave to her) to her (in other words, let the harlot keep the articles I gave her and allow the act to die in silence), lest we be shamed: behold, I sent this kid, and thou hast not found her (the whore).

24) And it came to pass about three months after, that it was told Judah, saying, Tamar thy daughter in law hath played the harlot; and also, behold, she is with child by whoredom. And Judah said, Bring her forth, and let her be burnt. (Judah plans on punishing Tamar by putting her to death)

25) When she (Tamar) was brought forth, she (Tamar) sent to her father in law, saying, By the man, whose these are, am I with child: and she (Tamar) said, Discern (think), I pray thee, whose are these, the signet, and bracelets, and staff.

26) And Judah acknowledged them (the articles), and said, She hath been more righteous than I; because that I gave her not to Shelah my son. (Now remember the scripture above when I said, 'Judah is very wicked.' **If a daughter in law who plays a harlot and conceives the father in laws child is more righteous than the father in law because the father in law does not give the daughter in law the father in law's youngest son to marry after that son is of age, then Judah must be very wicked, more wicked than the daughter in law who played the harlot and conceived a child from the father in law) And he (Judah) knew her again no more.** (Judah never laid with Tamar again. By all rights, Judah was Tamar's husband after Judah laid with Tamar and especially when Tamar conceived Judah's child. Then you would have a father in law and daughter in law being a husband and wife. I wouldn't laugh, this actually happens right

in the United States of America, then it's hidden and everyone wonders why God curses their offspring. God curses their offspring because they committed abominations and the three to four generation curse goes into effect. Heavenly Angel Lay Lay explains 'the three to four generation curse' in detail in my book, 'MATTHEW'S WORD 'TWO':REAL WORD OF GOD BIBLE')

27) And it came to pass in the time of her (Tamar) travail (delivery), that, behold, twins were in her (Tamar's) womb. (Judah is a father again, this time with Tamar having twins. This is wicked)

28) And it came to pass, when she (Tamar) travailed (delivered), that the one put out his hand (one of the boys in Tamar's womb): and the midwife took and bound upon his hand a scarlet thread, saying, This came out first.

29) And it came to pass, as he (the boy with the scarlet thread around his hand) drew back his hand, that, behold, his brother came out: and she (the midwife) said, How hast thou broken forth? (Astonished that the second boy actually came out of Tamar's womb first) this breach be upon thee: therefore his name was called Pharez. **(the second son is blamed and already cursed from birth for coming out first)**

30) And afterward came out his brother, that had the scarlet thread upon his hand: and his name was called Zarah. (the first son came out second)

GENESIS 39:1-23

1) And Joseph was brought down to Egypt; and Potiphar, an officer of Pharaoh, captain of the guard, an Egyptian, bought him of the hands of the Ishmeelites, which had brought him down thither. (Joseph was sold by the Ishmeelites to Potiphar)

2) And the Lord was with Joseph, and he (Joseph) was a prosperous man; and he was in the house of his master the Egyptian.

3) And his (Joseph's) master saw that the Lord was with him (Joseph), and that the Lord made all that he (Joseph) did to prosper in his (Joseph's) hand.

4) And Joseph found grace in his (Potiphar's) sight, and he (Joseph) served him (Potiphar): and he (Potiphar) made him (Joseph) overseer over his (Potiphar's) house, and all that he (Potiphar) had he (Potiphar) put into his (Joseph's) hand.

5) And it came to pass from the time that he (Potiphar) had made him (Joseph) overseer in his (Potiphar's) house, and over all that he (Potiphar) had, that the Lord blessed the Egyptian's house for Joseph's sake; and the blessing of the Lord was upon all that he (Potiphar) had in the house, and in the field.

6) And he (Potiphar) left all that he (Potiphar) had in Joseph's hand; and he (Potiphar) knew not ought he (Potiphar) had, save the bread which he did eat. (in other words, Potiphar had no idea how much wealth he had, Joseph was in charge of it all and God kept blessing Potiphar for Joseph's sake. Potiphar accumulated so much, he literally lost track of all his possessions and wealth) And Joseph was a goodly person, and well favoured.

7) And it came to pass after these things (this is very important, it's always after the man is in charge of great amounts of things or owns great amounts of things that a woman want that man to lay with her. Before then, the man is just another man), that his master's wife (Potiphar's wife) cast her eyes upon (looked seductively at) Joseph; and she said, Lie with me. (Potiphar's wife wants Joseph to have sex with her)

8) But he (Joseph) refused, and said unto his master's wife, Behold, my master wotteth not what is with me in the house (trusts me in his house), and he hath committed all that he hath to my hand;

9) There is none greater in this house than I; neither hath he (Potiphar) kept back any thing from me but thee (Joseph's master, Potiphar gave Joseph access to and rule over everything that Potiphar had except Potiphar's wife), because thou art his wife: how then can I do this great wickedness, and sin against God?

10) And it came to pass, as she (Potiphar's wife) spake to Joseph day by day, that he (Joseph) hearkened not (didn't listen to) unto her (Joseph did not listen to her or do as she kept asking Joseph to do to her), to lie by her, or to be with her.

11) And it came to pass about this time, that Joseph went into the house to do his business (Joseph had to go to the bathroom); and there was none of the men of the house there within (no one was in the house except Joseph and Potiphar's wife).

12) And she caught him (Joseph) by his garment (if Joseph wasn't using the bathroom, she wouldn't have gotten Joseph's garment to begin with), saying, Lie with me (have sex with me): and he (Joseph) left his garment (clothes) in her hand, and fled, and got him out.

13) And it came to pass, when she (Potiphar's wife) saw that he (Joseph) had left his (Joseph's) garment in her hand, and was fled forth (left the house),

14) That she (Potiphar's wife) called (screamed with a loud voice) unto the men of her house, and spake unto them, saying, See, he (Potiphar) hath brought in an Hebrew unto us to mock us; he (Joseph) came in unto me to lie with me, and I cried with a loud voice (lying woman, making things up when she doesn't get her way):

15) And it came to pass, when he (Joseph) heard that I lifted up my voice and cried (screamed for 'help'), that he (Joseph) left his garment with me, and fled, and got him out (Joseph left the house).

16) And she (Potiphar's wife) laid up his garment (Joseph's clothes) by her, until his (Joseph's master, Potiphar) lord came home.

17) And she (Potiphar's wife) spake unto him (Potiphar) according to these words, saying, The Hebrew servant (Joseph), which thou hast brought unto us, came in unto me to mock me (have sex with me):

18) And it came to pass, as I lifted up my voice and cried, that he (Joseph) left his garment with me, and fled out. (she is accusing Joseph of things Joseph was actually preventing just because she wanted Joseph to have sex with her)

19) And it came to pass, when his (Joseph's) master heard the words of his wife, which she spake unto him, saying, After this manner did thy servant (your servant, Joseph) to me (Potiphar is accepting what his wife is telling him at face value (with an

honest wife, that would be good, but I must wonder if Joseph is the only man Potiphar's wife wanted to have sex with, I'm sure by her actions she has been laid by other men in the kingdom other than her own husband. This action had to have started somewhere and Potiphar's wife has gotten away with it time and time again); that his (Potiphar's) wrath was kindled (Potiphar got extremely angry, as any man would be if their wife was approached by other men for sex).

20) And Joseph's master took him, and put him (Joseph) into the prison, a place where the king's prisoners were bound: and he (Joseph) was there in the prison. (**Contrary to Hollywood movies where Potiphar asks Joseph what really happens and Joseph tells Potiphar. Just like Heavenly Angel Lay Lay said, 'Hollywood downplays the King James Version of the Word of God'. Potiphar didn't ask Joseph anything, Potiphar took the word of his wife and persecuted Joseph for something Joseph didn't even do. That sounds like a lot of the men who loose their children because the woman lies to the officials, telling the officials the man does things the man really isn't doing and the officials automatically believe the woman**)

21) But the Lord was with Joseph, and shewed him mercy, and gave him favour in the sight of the keeper of the prison.

22) And the keeper of the prison committed to Joseph's hand all the prisoners that were in the prison; and whatsoever they did there, he was the doer of it. (Joseph was in charge of the prison. See the Lord was with Joseph, just like the Lord is always with us, no matter where we are. The Lord went to prison with Joseph)

23) The keeper of the prison looked not to any thing that was under his hand (the keeper of the prison didn't worry about anything that Joseph was in charge of); because the Lord was with him (Joseph), and that which he (Joseph) did, the Lord made it to prosper.

GENESIS 40:1-23

1) And it came to pass after these things, that the butler of the king of Egypt and his baker had offended their lord the king of

Egypt.

2) And Pharaoh was wroth (angry) against two of his officers, against the chief of the butlers, and against the chief of the bakers.

3) And he (the Pharaoh) put them (the chief butler and the chief baker) in ward in the house of the captain of the guard, into the prison, the place where Joseph was bound.

4) And the captain of the guard charged (a highly intense situation) Joseph with them (Joseph was to serve the chief butler and chief baker), and he (Joseph) served them: and they continued a season in ward.

5) And they (the chief butler and chief baker) dreamed a dream both of them, each man his dream in one night, each man according to the interpretation of his dream, the butler and the baker of the king of Egypt, which were bound in the prison.

6) And Joseph came in unto them (the chief butler and chief baker) in the morning, and looked upon them, and, behold, they were sad.

7) And he (Joseph) asked Pharaoh's officers that were with him in the ward of his lord's house, saying, Wherefore look ye so sadly to day?

8) And they (the chief butler and chief baker) said unto him (Joseph), We have dreamed a dream, and there is no interpreter of it. And Joseph said unto them, Do not interpretations belong to God? tell me them (the dreams), I pray you.

9) And the chief butler told his dream to Joseph, and said to him (Joseph), In my dream, behold, a vine was before me;

10) And in the vine were three branches: and it was as though it budded, and her blossoms shot forth; and the clusters thereof brought forth ripe grapes:

11) And Pharaoh's cup was in my hand: and I took the grapes, and pressed them into Pharaoh's cup, and I gave the cup into Pharaoh's hand.

12) And Joseph said unto him, This is the interpretation of it: The three branches are three days:

13) Yet within three days shall Pharaoh lift up thine (your) head, and restore thee (you) unto thy (your) place: and thou (you) shalt

deliver Pharaoh's cup into his hand, after the former manner when thou wast his butler. (just like you did before)

14) But think on me when it shall be well with thee, and shew (show) kindness, I pray thee, unto me, and make mention of me unto Pharaoh, and bring me out of this house:

15) For indeed I was stolen away out of the land of the Hebrews: and here also have I done nothing that they should put me into the dungeon.

16) When the chief baker saw that the interpretation was good, he said unto Joseph, I also was in my dream, and, behold, I had three white baskets on my head:

17) And in the uppermost basket there was of all manner of bakemeats for Pharaoh; and the birds did eat them out of the basket upon my head.

18) And Joseph answered and said, This is the interpretation thereof: The three baskets are three days:

19) Yet within three days shall Pharaoh lift up thy (your) head from off thee (you), and shall hang thee (you) on a tree; and the birds shall eat thy (your) flesh from off thee (you).

20) And it came to pass the third day, which was Pharaoh's birthday, that he (the Pharaoh) made a feast unto all his servants: and he (the Pharaoh) lifted up the head of the chief butler and of the chief baker among his servants.

21) And he (the Pharaoh) restored the chief butler unto his butlership again; and he (the butler) gave the cup into Pharaoh's hand:

22) But he (the Pharaoh) hanged the chief baker: as Joseph had interpreted to them.

23) Yet did not the chief butler remember Joseph, but forgat him.

GENESIS 41:1-57

1) And it came to pass at the end of two full years, that Pharaoh dreamed: and, behold, he (Pharaoh) stood by the river.

2) And, behold, there came up out of the river seven well favoured kine (cows) and fat fleshed; and they fed in a meadow.

3) And, behold, seven other kine (cows) came up after them out of the river, ill favoured and lean fleshed; and stood by the other

kine (cows) upon the brink of the river.

4) And the ill favoured and lean fleshed kine (cows) did eat up the seven well favoured and fat kine (cows). So Pharaoh awoke.

5) And he (Pharaoh) slept and dreamed the second time: and, behold, seven ears of corn came up upon one stalk, rank and good.

6) And, behold, seven thin ears and blasted with the east wind sprung up after them.

7) And the seven thin ears devoured the seven rank and full ears. And Pharaoh awoke, and, behold, it was a dream.

8) And it came to pass in the morning that his spirit was troubled; and he sent and called for all the magicians of Egypt, and all the wise men thereof: and Pharaoh told them his dream; but there was none that could interpret them (the dreams) unto Pharaoh.

9) Then spake the chief butler unto Pharaoh, saying, I do remember my faults this day:

10) Pharaoh was wroth (angry) with his servants, and put me in ward in the captain of the guard's house, both me and the chief baker:

11) And we dreamed a dream in one night, I and he; we dreamed each man according to the interpretation of his dream.

12) And there was there with us a young man, an Hebrew, servant to the captain of the guard; and we told him, and he interpreted to us our dreams; to each man according to his dream he did interpret.

13) And it came to pass, as he (the Hebrew) interpreted to us, so it was; me (the chief butler) he (the Pharaoh) restored unto mine office, and him (the chief baker) he (the Pharaoh) hanged.

14) Then Pharaoh sent and called Joseph, and they brought him (Joseph) hastily out of the dungeon: and he (Joseph) shaved himself, and changed his raiment, and came in unto Pharaoh.

15) And Pharaoh said unto Joseph, I have dreamed a dream, and there is none that can interpret it: and I have heard say of thee (you), that thou (you) canst understand a dream to interpret it.

16) And Joseph answered Pharaoh, saying, It is not in me: God shall give Pharaoh an answer of peace.

17) And Pharaoh said unto Joseph, In my dream, behold, I stood

upon the bank of the river:

18) And, behold, there came up out of the river seven kine (cows), fat fleshed and well favoured; and they fed in a meadow:

19) And, behold, seven other kine (cows) came up after them, poor and very ill favoured and lean fleshed, such as I never saw in all the land of Egypt for badness:

20) And the lean and the ill favoured kine (cows) did eat up the first seven fat kine (cows):

21) And when they (the lean cows) had eaten them up (the fat cows), it could not be known that they (the thin cows) had eaten them (the fat cows); but they (the thin cows) were still ill favoured (thin), as at the beginning. So I awoke.

22) And I saw in my dream, and, behold, seven ears came up in one stalk, full and good:

23) And, behold, seven ears, withered, thin, and blasted with the east wind, sprung up after them:

24) And the thin ears devoured the seven good ears: and I told this unto the magicians; but there was none that could declare it to me. (I need to say here that contrary to movies about the bible when you see Joseph not only telling the Pharaoh what the dreams are but also interpreting the dreams. If you have read my book MATTHEW'S WORD 'TWO':REAL WORD OF GOD BIBLE, you will remember that Heavenly Angel Lay Lay did say, 'Don't listen to Hollywood when it comes to the Word of God. Hollywood has taken the Word of God, distorted it, and downplayed it to fit Satan's agenda')

25) And Joseph said unto Pharaoh, The dream of Pharaoh is one: God hath shewed Pharaoh what he (God) is about to do.

26) The seven good kine (cows) are seven years; and the seven good ears are seven years: the dream is one.

27) And the seven thin and ill favoured kine (cows) that came up after them are seven years; and the seven empty ears blasted with the east wind shall be seven years of famine.

28) This is the thing which I have spoken unto Pharaoh: What God is about to do he (God) sheweth (showed) unto Pharaoh.

29) Behold, there come seven years of great plenty throughout all the land of Egypt:

30) And there shall arise after them seven years of famine; and all the plenty shall be forgotten in the land of Egypt; and the famine shall consume the land;

31) And the plenty shall not be known in the land by reason of that famine following; for it shall be very grievous.

32) And for that the dream was doubled unto Pharaoh twice; it is because the thing is established by God, and God will shortly bring it to pass.

33) Now therefore let Pharaoh look out a man discreet and wise, and set him over the land of Egypt.

34) Let Pharaoh do this, and let him appoint officers over the land, and take up the fifth part of the land of Egypt in the seven plenteous years.

35) And let them (the man and officers appointed over the land) gather all the food of those good years that come, and lay up corn under the hand of Pharaoh, and let them keep food in the cities.

36) And that food shall be for store to the land against the seven years of famine, which shall be in the land of Egypt; that the land perish not through the famine.

37) And the thing was good in the eyes of Pharaoh, and in the eyes of all his servants.

38) And Pharaoh said unto his servants, Can we find such a one as this is, a man in whom the Spirit of God is?

39) And Pharaoh said unto Joseph, Forasmuch as God hath shewed (showed) thee (you) all this, there is none so discreet and wise as thou art (you are):

40) Thou shalt be over my house, and according unto thy word shall all my people be ruled: only in the throne will I be greater than thou.

41) And Pharaoh said unto Joseph, See, I have set thee over all the land of Egypt.

42) And Pharaoh took off his ring from his hand, and put it upon Joseph's hand, and arrayed him in vestures of fine linen, and put a gold chain about his neck;

43) And he (Pharaoh) made him (Joseph) to ride in the second chariot which he had; and they (Pharaoh's men) cried before him (Joseph), Bow the knee: and he (Pharaoh) made him (Joseph)

ruler over all the land of Egypt.

44) And Pharaoh said unto Joseph, I am Pharaoh, and without thee (you) shall no man lift up his hand or foot in all the land of Egypt. (Joseph's dreams coming true)

45) And Pharaoh called Joseph's name Zaphnathpaaneah; and he gave him to wife Asenath the daughter of Potipherah priest of On. And Joseph went out over all the land of Egypt.

46) And Joseph was thirty years old when he stood before Pharaoh king of Egypt. And Joseph went out from the presence of Pharaoh, and went throughout all the land of Egypt.

47) And in the seven plenteous years the earth brought forth by handfuls.

48) And he (Joseph) gathered up all the food of the seven years, which were in the land of Egypt, and laid up the food in the cities: the food of the field, which was round about every city, laid he (Joseph) up in the same.

49) And Joseph gathered corn as the sand of the sea, very much, until he left numbering; for it was without number.

50) And unto Joseph were born two sons before the years of famine came, which Asenath the daughter of Potipherah priest of On bare unto him.

51) And Joseph called the name of the firstborn Manasseh: For God, said he, hath made me forget all my toil, and all my father's house.

52) And the name of the second called he Ephraim: For God hath caused me to be fruitful in the land of my affliction.

53) And the seven years of plenteousness, that was in the land of Egypt, were ended.

54) And the seven years of dearth (famine)began to come, according as Joseph had said: and the dearth (famine) was in all lands; but in all the land of Egypt there was bread.

55) And when all the land of Egypt was famished, the people cried to Pharaoh for bread: and Pharaoh said unto all the Egyptians, Go unto Joseph; what he saith to you, do.

56) And the famine was over all the face of the earth: and Joseph opened all the storehouses, and sold unto the Egyptians; and the famine waxed sore in the land of Egypt.

57) And all countries came into Egypt to Joseph for to buy corn; because that the famine was so sore in all lands.

GENESIS 42:1-38

1) Now when Jacob saw that there was corn in Egypt, Jacob said unto his sons, Why do ye look one upon another?

2) And he said, Behold, I have heard that there is corn in Egypt: get you down thither (go down to Egypt), and buy for us from thence (there); that we may live, and not die. (Go down to Egypt and buy corn from the Egyptians that we may live)

3) And Joseph's ten brethren went down to buy corn in Egypt.

4) But Benjamin, Joseph's brother, Jacob sent not with his brethren; for he (Jacob) said, Lest peradventure mischief befall him (Benjamin).

5) And the sons of Israel came to buy corn among those that came: for the famine was in the land of Canaan.

6) And Joseph was the governor over the land, and he it was that sold to all the people of the land: and Joseph's brethren came, and bowed down themselves before him with their faces to the earth. (Joseph's dreams coming true)

7) And Joseph saw his brethren, and he knew them, but made himself strange unto them, and spake roughly unto them; and he said unto them, Whence come ye? And they said, From the land of Canaan to buy food.

8) And Joseph knew his brethren, but they (Joseph's brothers) knew not him (Joseph).

9) And Joseph remembered the dreams which he dreamed of them, and said unto them, Ye are spies; to see the nakedness (bareness) of the land ye are come.

10) And they said unto him, Nay, my lord (Joseph's brothers bowing down to Joseph and calling Joseph 'lord'. Just as Joseph dreamed would happen), but to buy food are thy servants come.

11) We are all one man's sons; we are true men, thy (your) servants are no spies.

12) And he (Joseph) said unto them (the brothers), Nay, but to see the nakedness of the land ye (you) are come.

13) And they (Joseph's brothers) said, Thy (your) servants are

twelve brethren, the sons of one man in the land of Canaan; and, behold, the youngest is this day with our father, and one is not.

14) And Joseph said unto them, That is it that I spake unto you, saying, Ye are spies:

15) Hereby ye shall be proved: By the life of Pharaoh ye shall not go forth hence, except your youngest brother come hither. (Joseph wants Benjamin to come to him)

16) Send one of you, and let him (the one selected) fetch your brother (Benjamin), and ye shall be kept in prison, that your words may be proved, whether there be any truth in you: or else by the life of Pharaoh surely ye (you) are spies.

17) And he (Joseph) put them (his brothers) all together into ward three days.

18) And Joseph said unto them the third day, This do, and live; for I fear God:

19) If ye be true men, let one of your brethren be bound in the house of your prison: go ye, carry corn for the famine of your houses: (all of the brothers can go, but one. One must stay in prison for the return of the youngest brother. We aren't talking about a few days here, On, Egypt to Kadesh-Barnea is 175 miles or 292.25 kilometers north and Kadesh-Barnea to Hebron is about 75 miles or 125 kilometers north. 175+75=250 miles or 417.25 kilometers north at 25 miles a day by camel, but also wagons etc that Joseph was sending with his brothers full of corn, so the time would be longer. 250/25=10 days/6=at least 1.7 weeks travel each way. Remember six days for a week because the seventh day everyone rested)

20) But bring your youngest brother unto me; so shall your words be verified, and ye shall not die. And they did so. (Joseph's brothers did as they were told)

21) And they (Joseph's brothers) said one to another, We are verily guilty concerning our brother (Joseph), in that we saw the anguish of his (Joseph's) soul, when he besought us, and we would not hear; therefore is this distress come upon us.

22) And Reuben answered them, saying, Spake I not unto you, saying, Do not sin against the child; and ye (you) would not hear? therefore, behold, also his (Benjamin's) blood is required.

23) And they (Joseph's brothers) knew not that Joseph understood them; for he spake unto them by an interpreter.

24) And he turned himself about from them (Joseph turned away from his brothers), and wept; and returned to them (the brothers) again, and communed with them (the brothers), and took from them Simeon, and bound him (Simeon) before their (the brothers) eyes.

25) Then Joseph commanded to fill their sacks with corn, and to restore every man's money into his sack, and to give them provision (food) for the way: and thus did he (Joseph) unto them (the brothers).

26) And they laded (loaded) their asses with the corn, and departed thence (left then).

27) And as one of them opened his sack to give his ass provender (food) in the inn, he espied (spotted) his money; for, behold, it was in his sack's mouth.

28) And he said unto his brethren, My money is restored; and, lo, it is even in my sack: and their heart failed them, and they were afraid, saying one to another, What is this that God hath done unto us?

29) And they came unto Jacob their father unto the land of Canaan, and told him all that befell unto them; saying,

30) The man, who is the lord of the land, spake roughly to us, and took us for spies of the country.

31) And we said unto him, We are true men; we are no spies:

32) We be twelve brethren, sons of our father; one is not, and the youngest is this day with our father in the land of Canaan.

33) And the man, the lord of the country, said unto us, Hereby shall I know that ye are true men; leave one of your brethren here with me, and take food for the famine of your households, and be gone:

34) And bring your youngest brother unto me: then shall I know that ye are no spies, but that ye are true men: so will I deliver you your brother, and ye shall traffick in the land.

35) And it came to pass as they emptied their sacks, that, behold, every man's bundle of money was in his sack: and when both they and their father saw the bundles of money, they were afraid.

36) And Jacob their father said unto them, Me have ye bereaved of my children: Joseph is not, and Simeon is not, and ye will take Benjamin away: all these things are against me.

37) And Reuben spake unto his father, saying, Slay my two sons, if I bring him (Benjamin) not to thee (Jacob): (in other words, Reuben is telling Jacob if Reuben doesn't deliver Benjamin back to Jacob, then Jacob can slay Reuben's two sons) deliver him (Benjamin) into my (Reuben's) hand, and I will bring him (Benjamin) to thee (Jacob) again.

38) And he (Jacob) said, My son (Benjamin) shall not go down with you; for his (Benjamin's) brother is dead, and he (Benjamin) is left alone: if mischief befall him (Benjamin) by the way in the which ye (you) go, then shall ye (you) bring down my gray hairs with sorrow to the grave (Jacob is saying if anything happened to Benjamin, Jacob would die. Jacob couldn't handle Benjamin dieing too. Jacob had already lost Joseph and now Simeon).

**(CONTINUED IN: HEAVENLY ANGEL LAY LAY
EXPLAINS WHY GAYS, LESBIANS AND
TRANSSEXUALS
DO NOT GO TO HEAVEN)**

BIBLIOGRAPHY

1.   Encarta ® World English Dictionary © & (P) 1998-2004 Microsoft Corporation. All rights reserved.

2. Merriam Webster's Collegiate Dictionary Tenth Edition (1993), United States of America.

3. The Holy Bible King James Version (1998), B. B. Kirkbride Bible Co., Inc. Indianapolis, IN..USA